THE LANGUAGE ARCHIVE

BY JULIA CHO

DRAMATISTS
PLAY SERVICE
INC.

THE LANGUAGE ARCHIVE
Copyright © 2012, Julia Cho

All Rights Reserved

THE LANGUAGE ARCHIVE is fully protected under the copyright laws of the United States of America, and of all countries covered by the International Copyright Union (including the Dominion of Canada and the rest of the British Commonwealth), and of all countries covered by the Pan-American Copyright Convention, the Universal Copyright Convention, the Berne Convention, and of all countries with which the United States has reciprocal copyright relations. No part of this publication may be reproduced in any form by any means (electronic, mechanical, photocopying, recording, or otherwise), or stored in any retrieval system in any way (electronic or mechanical) without written permission of the publisher.

The English language stock and amateur stage performance rights in the United States, its territories, possessions and Canada for THE LANGUAGE ARCHIVE are controlled exclusively by Dramatists Play Service, 440 Park Avenue South, New York, NY 10016. **No professional or nonprofessional performance of the Play may be given without obtaining in advance the written permission of Dramatists Play Service and paying the requisite fee.**

All other rights, including without limitation motion picture, recitation, lecturing, public reading, radio broadcasting, television, video or sound recording, and the rights of translation into foreign languages are strictly reserved.

Inquiries concerning all other rights should be addressed to WME Entertainment, 11 Madison Avenue, New York, NY 10010. Attn: John Buzzetti.

NOTE ON BILLING

Anyone receiving permission to produce THE LANGUAGE ARCHIVE is required to give credit to the Author as sole and exclusive Author of the Play on the title page of all programs distributed in connection with performances of the Play and in all instances in which the title of the Play appears, including printed or digital materials for advertising, publicizing or otherwise exploiting the Play and/or a production thereof. The name of the Author must appear on a separate line, in which no other name appears, immediately beneath the title and in size of type equal to 50% of the size of the largest, most prominent letter used for the title of the Play. No person, firm or entity may receive credit larger or more prominent than that accorded the Author. The following acknowledgments must appear on the title page in all programs distributed in connection with performances of the Play:

Commissioned and Originally Produced by Roundabout Theatre Company,
New York, NY, Todd Haimes, Artistic Director.

The Language Archive received its world premiere at South Coast Repertory, produced by special arrangement with Roundabout Theatre Company.

The Language Archive's development was supported by
the Eugene O'Neill Theatre Center during a residency at
the National Playwrights Conference 2009.

SPECIAL NOTE ON EPIGRAPH

Reprinted from *6,000 Years of Bread* by special arrangement with Skyhorse Publishing, Inc.

SPECIAL NOTE ON SONGS/RECORDINGS

Dramatists Play Service neither holds the rights to nor grants permission to use any songs or recordings mentioned in the Play. Permission for performances of copyrighted songs, arrangements or recordings mentioned in this Play is not included in our license agreement. The permission of the copyright owner(s) must be obtained for any such use. For any songs and/or recordings mentioned in the Play, other songs, arrangements, or recordings may be substituted provided permission from the copyright owner(s) of such songs, arrangements or recordings is obtained; or songs, arrangements or recordings in the public domain may be substituted.

THE LANGUAGE ARCHIVE was produced at the Roundabout Theatre's Harold and Miriam Steinberg Center for Theatre in New York City, opening on October 17, 2010. It was directed by Mark Brokaw; the set design was by Neil Patel; the costume design was by Michael Krass; the lighting design was by Marc McCullogh; the original music and sound design were by David Van Tieghem; the dialect coach was Ben Furey; and the stage manager was William H. Lang. The cast was as follows:

GEORGE	Matt Letscher
MARY	Heidi Schreck
EMMA	Betty Gilpin
ALTA	Jayne Houdyshell
RESTEN	John Horton

THE LANGUAGE ARCHIVE received its world premiere at South Coast Repertory, produced by special arrangement with Roundabout Theatre Company. It was directed by Mark Brokaw; the set design was by Neil Patel; the costume design was by Rachel Myers; the lighting design was by Marc McCullogh; the original music and sound design were by Steven Cahill; the dialect coach was Phillip D. Thompson; and the stage manager was Chrissy Church. The cast was as follows:

GEORGE	Leo Marks
MARY	Betsy Brandt
EMMA	Laura Heisler
ALTA	Linda Gehringer
RESTEN	Tony Amendola

CHARACTERS

GEORGE: A linguist. A man in his 30s or 40s.

MARY: George's wife. A woman in her 30s or 40s.

EMMA: A lab assistant. A woman in her 20s or 30s.

ALTA: An old woman.

RESTEN: An old man.

(The actors playing Alta and Resten could also play the following:)

THE DRIVER: A man of any age.

OLD MAN/BAKER: An old man.

LANGUAGE INSTRUCTOR: A woman of any age.

A PASSERBY: A man or a woman of any age.

A PASSERBY: A man or a woman of any age (different from the previous).

CONDUCTOR: A man or a woman of any age.

OLD MAN/ZAMENHOF: An old man.

"Why should I take up such a burden?" I thought to myself. "Who would ever finish gathering so much material?" But then I did take up the burden. And I gathered — without finishing.

And now, in the midst of the gathering, I begin the tale.

—H.E. Jacob
Six Thousand Years of Bread

THE LANGUAGE ARCHIVE

ACT ONE

Scene 1

George and Mary.

GEORGE. Lately, I've become worried about my wife. She used to be an upbeat person. But recently, she's become very sad. She cries at everything — long-distance phone commercials, nature specials when animals of prey get killed, sometimes over nothing at all —
MARY. Um … George?
GEORGE. — She'll just be washing the dishes and then suddenly slump over.
MARY. George, I can hear you. I'm right here.
GEORGE. I'm just trying to explain how you've been lately.
MARY. How *I've* been?
GEORGE. Yes. The … your tendency lately to be kind of … sad.
MARY. Well, that's very funny. Kind of hilarious, actually, because from my viewpoint, you're the one who's sad.
GEORGE. Me?
MARY. You.
GEORGE. That's ridiculous — why should I be — why should you think I'm sad? I don't cry, I don't carry on —
MARY. Exactly, that's th —
GEORGE. You're the one who can't stop crying. *(To us.)* She cries when she makes salad, she cries when she swiffs the floor, she cries

when she pays the bills and then she uses her *tears* to seal the envelopes —

MARY. But I —

GEORGE. She even cries — she even cries when she's asleep. She wakes up in the morning and there are little pools of tears in her ears, she stands up and they trickle down her neck and become little pools in her collarbones and where are you going? *(Mary has left. To us.)* And then she goes. She never wants to talk about it. No matter. It's not like I don't have other things to attend to. There are many developments in my field that I must constantly keep abreast of. Too many, in fact. The task: it's quite Sisyphean. *(There is an armchair and beside it, a towering pile of books. George sits and opens a book. He flips a page. He finds a small piece of paper tucked into the book. He takes it out. He reads it. He is perplexed.)* Mary? *(Mary enters. She has the aspect of having been interrupted right in the middle of something — some piece of housework.)*

MARY. Yes?

GEORGE. Mary, do you know what this is?

MARY. What is what?

GEORGE. *(Reading.)* "Husband or throw pillow? Wife or hot water bottle? Marriage or an old cardigan? Love or explaining how to use the remote control?"

MARY. What is that?

GEORGE. I'm asking you. It was in my book.

MARY. That's odd.

GEORGE. Right here, in my book. It's a new book.

MARY. Is it a bookmark?

GEORGE. It's written on a scrap of paper.

MARY. Maybe some bookstore worker put it there.

GEORGE. It's in your handwriting, Mary.

MARY. I don't know what you mean. *(She leaves. George goes back to reading. He takes a sip from a mug of tea by his elbow. He drains it, then does a slight double take. He lifts out his tea bag. He sees at the bottom of the mug.)*

GEORGE. "In a moment of sadness, sitting on the last, lowest note, she knew they both saw the fragility of their marriage when he said: 'Maybe we should try ballroom dancing.'" *(Calling.)* Mary. *(Mary enters. George pulls out the wet piece of paper from the bottom of the mug.)* What does this mean? *(Mary goes over, takes the wet piece of paper and reads it.)*

MARY. I have no idea.
GEORGE. I know you put this here.
MARY. This couldn't possibly be me. You've never suggested ballroom dancing.
GEORGE. So someone else has crept into our house —
MARY. There are people, you know, / who go into houses and take ladies' underwear, so —
GEORGE. — and put a note into my book, my tea? *(Registering what she's said.)* Yes, "take" operative word. Not leave behind — *(He reads.)* "The fragility of their marriage." What is that? What does that mean?
MARY. These notes aren't from me, how many times do I have to say it?
GEORGE. Just admit it, admit you're going around leaving bad poetry lying around the house —
MARY. IT ISN'T ME. *(She leaves.)*
GEORGE. Now. My wife is not one to lie. Neither is she one to write poetry. If that's even what these notes are. It seems quite impossible that she is the one leaving these for me to find. And yet. She is the only other person in this house besides me. And so: I thought: maybe: I can catch her in the act. *(George spies on Mary. Mary is in the kitchen, washing dishes. She wears bright yellow rubber gloves. She begins to cry. It starts off with a tear trickling down her face. Then a few more. A few sniffles. She slumps over. It's not a big crying jag. But there is no doubt that she is crying. Weeping. She tries to wipe her tears on the bit of sleeve not covered by the rubber glove. She sighs. She collects herself. And then she resumes washing dishes as if nothing has happened. George is unsure whether to stay or go.)* ... Mary ... ?
MARY. Have you figured it out?
GEORGE. No. But I wanted to, that is, perhaps we could discuss ...
MARY. Discuss ...?
GEORGE. This habit of yours, this phase ... perhaps you could use ... help.
MARY. Well, now that you mention it, it would be nice if you could vacuum the stairs —
GEORGE. I meant help with other issues.
MARY. What issues?
GEORGE. Well, the ... crying, among other things; I don't think — I could be wrong, but I highly doubt it — that it's normal to be this way —

MARY. Oh, you'd rather I be *your* way?
GEORGE. What way?
MARY. Well. I just find it odd, a little, don't you think, that we've been together now for how many years and I've never seen you cry. Not once.
GEORGE. Is that all?
MARY. When we watch the news, I'm weeping and all you do is continue to read — earthquakes, massacres, it doesn't matter, you read —
GEORGE. We've spoken about this — the magnitude, it numbs you, lots of people have the same — it's our inability as humans, large tragedies overwhelm us —
MARY. When Cookie died, you didn't even want to go to the vet —
GEORGE. She was *your* dog! She never even liked me!
MARY. And I should've known something was wrong when your grandmother passed away and everyone else was bawling but you didn't even shed a tear —
GEORGE. Well, she was *old*. And it's not like we were — you know — close. I mean we didn't even speak the same language.
MARY. But still, the human reaction, the normal reaction, is to mourn.
GEORGE. I do mourn. I mourn a lot.
MARY. You mourn ideas. Not people.
GEORGE. Cookie wasn't a person!
MARY. SHE WAS TO ME.
GEORGE. I just don't find death, a single human — or canine — death, a tragedy, I'm sorry. Because we all die. It's not like something unnatural happening. It's not like when my grandmother died it was a surprise. I mean, she'd been sick a long time, she was an old woman and she died — what, I should be … / devastated —
MARY. I'm leaving you.
GEORGE. What? *(Mary is very, very still. George is very, very still.)* What did you say? *(To us.)* At this point, I'm thinking I must've misheard her, that this is all some kind of misunderstanding and that we can go on, just as before — she could lie, is what I'm saying, and pretend the words that just came out of her mouth did not just come out of her mouth —
MARY. *(Bravely, simply, with an amount of wonder.)* I'm leaving you.
GEORGE. But she doesn't. And they do.

MARY. I'm. Leaving. *(A long pause. George stares at Mary. Mary stares at George. Lights shift.)*
GEORGE. It's a very curious thing when your wife leaves you. The world slows down. Words become … *(Lugubriously.)* lugubrious.
MARY. I'mmmleeevvinnnngyyyyooooooo …
GEORGE. My heart was beating very loudly. But instead of thumping, every beat was saying, "Take it back, take it back, take it back." Just like that. Like a rhythm. And it was so loud that I couldn't hear anything else, even my own thoughts, whatever they might have been. And I was sure she must be hearing it too. It was as thunderous as horse hooves, louder than tanks, how could anyone not hear it? Take it back, take it back, take it back. Or if she couldn't hear it, I thought surely she must be able to see it, the words running like ticker tape through the whites of my eyes, like those old cartoons when the cat is hit on the head with a mallet. Take it back, take it back. My whole body was begging her. Take it back, take it back — If you go, it'll destroy me. Take it back, take it back — I'll be a city in ruins — Take it back, take it back — It's not too late — Take it back, take it back — My whole body was shouting it. Couldn't SHE HEAR IT? Why wasn't she saying something?
MARY. George?
GEORGE. Yes?
MARY. … Well? *(Pause.)* Don't you have anything to say? *(Silence. George struggles to speak.)*
GEORGE. … Don't … Go…? *(Mary sighs. She goes.)*

Scene 2

George.

GEORGE. I am a linguist. This is my trade. Lots of people ask me if this means I can speak a lot of languages. And I do have a passable acquaintance with Greek, Latin, French, Cantonese, Spanish, Dutch, Portuguese and Esperanto. Of these all, I am perhaps most fond of Esperanto, that made-up, utopian dream of a language. Proudly, I say, "*La vivo sen Esperanto estas neimagebla al mi!*" Life without Esperanto is unimaginable to me! So. What is death to a linguist? What is, so to speak, worth mourning? I know this: There are sixty-nine hundred languages in the world. More than half are expected to die within the next century. In fact, it's estimated that every two weeks, a language dies. I don't know about you, but this statistic moves me far more than any statistic on how many animals die or people die in a given time, in a given place. Because when we say a language dies, we are talking about a whole world, a whole way of life. It is the death of imagination, of memory. It makes me much sadder than I could ever possibly express. Even with all my languages, there still aren't the right words.

Scene 3

The Lab.

Emma readies the instruments. Among them, there is a computer attached to a recording device. The device has many complicated wires and knobs. Emma makes a few, last adjustments just as George enters.

EMMA. Morning, George.
GEORGE. Morning, Emma.
EMMA. How was your weekend?
GEORGE. Fine. It was ... what are we doing today?
EMMA. The Ellowans are here.
GEORGE. The who?
EMMA. The Ellowans, George, you've been looking forward to them all month.
GEORGE. The Ellowans, yes, of course, how are they?
EMMA. They're fine. They wanted breakfast and so I took them to an IHOP. Now they're waiting in the lounge. George.
GEORGE. Mm?
EMMA. Is everything ok? You seem a bit ...
GEORGE. I apologize. I will focus. The Ellowans. *(He fiddles around with the machine. We might notice Emma gazing at him with a soft look in her eyes. Into a microphone.)* Testing, testing. 1-2-3. *(He presses a button and his voice returns, clear as a bell.)* Testing, testing. 1-2-3. *(He turns to Emma. The soft look in her eyes covers itself just in time.)* You fixed it.
EMMA. I did.
GEORGE. You're simply amazing, Emma, do you know that? *(Emma smiles. It's the kind of smile that seems small, but inside it's enormous.)* Show them in, please.
EMMA. Of course. *(Emma leaves. For a moment, sadness overtakes George. His body slumps. His face is ashen.)*
EMMA. *(Offstage.)* Right this way. *(George takes a deep breath, straightens his back and composes a pleasant face. The door opens.)*

GEORGE. Come in, come in. *(Emma enters with Alta and Resten They are old — it's impossible to say how old — and dressed in layered clothes that seem almost haphazard, although very neat. They seem foreign but it's hard to place how.)* Welcome, welcome to The Language Archive. *(George greets them, shakes their hands.)* It's an honor to have you both here. How was the flight?

Scene 4

Mary. She is packing.

MARY. I am not depressed. First of all. I think you should know that. Depression, to me, is numbness: the absence of emotion. My husband sees me bow my head and weep and thinks that this is depression. Sadness, he calls it. My husband is very reductive. What he does not know — because he has not cried probably since he was seven and broke a limb or something — what he does not know is that there are many reasons for weeping. There is the: I can't believe how beautiful it is, so I weep. Or the: I can't believe how true it is, so I weep. Or: I can't believe I'm going to die someday, so I weep. Or: I can't believe everyone I love is going to die someday, so I weep. Or: I am marked for suffering, so I weep. Or: We are all marked for suffering, so I weep. *(By now her face is radiant. There are still tears on her face, but there is something like joy shining in her eyes. She composes herself and closes her suitcase. It clicks shut. She then takes out a small, folded piece of paper. She stuffs it into one of George's slippers. And then, without a backward glance, she goes.)*

Scene 5

The lab.

George gives Alta and Resten a brief tour.

GEORGE. Where we are now is the very heart of The Language Archive, a five-hundred-strong collection of priceless tapes and recordings. It is the last surviving remnant of worlds and cultures that no longer exist, of languages such as Arden, Potowtuck, Gissgin — and after this week, with your help, Elloway. This is the room in which we will be recording you. I can't tell you how excited we were to learn there were still some speakers of Elloway left — we thought the language died out in 1954. And the fact that you're married — usually when we get to the point where we have only one or two speakers, they're not even fluent; it's like a second or third language to them, half-remembered at best. Or we have only one speaker and they can only tell stories — long, unbroken soliloquies. But to be able to record actual conversation! It's just so exciting! I'm really quite beside myself. *(Alta shrugs. Resten shrugs.)* Well. Shall we begin? *(They all sit. George moves the microphone near Resten. George and Emma put on headphones. George nods to Emma. Emma starts recording.)* Whenever you're ready. *(Resten opens his mouth about to talk. Alta leans forward.)*
ALTA. I. Did. Not.
RESTEN. Yes you did.
ALTA. Did NOT.
RESTEN. DID SO, DID SO, DID SO. You did SO take up the entire armrest, which made it not so very comfortable, let me telling you!

ALTA.	GEORGE. *(Underneath.)*
Well, it was not FAIR that you made me sit in the middle, no one likes the middle, but who goes in the middle?	Excuse me … um … Excuse me…?

RESTEN. You wanting me to sit next to big guy with big shoulders, make me squeeze, you know I have weak heart —

ALTA. You do NOT, you just SAY you do because you are a worm, a lying worm, my life is like beautiful perfect apple, and then you are WORM who come in and eat the rotten heart —
RESTEN. YES, exactly — ROT-TON HEART you have —
GEORGE. *(Overlapping.)* Stop —
RESTEN. *(Overlapping.)* — And it's KILLING me, killing me every day!
GEORGE. STOP. Please. Stop the recording. *(A rest.)* I'm sorry, but is this — is this somehow for our benefit?
ALTA. Excuse?
GEORGE. That you're arguing in English. Is that for us? *(Alta and Resten look at each other. They chuckle.)*
RESTEN. No no no.
ALTA. That is a most silly assumption.
RESTEN. We are talking in English —
ALTA. Because English is the language of anger.
RESTEN. Only angry people speak it, only hard people.
ALTA. Yes. With guns.
RESTEN. And very bad manner.
ALTA. But our language —
RESTEN. Our language is too sacred for this kind of angry talk.
ALTA. Our language is the language of —
RESTEN. What would you call it?
ALTA. Our language is the language our parents filled into our ear —
RESTEN. At night, with susurrations —
ALTA. And whisperings —
RESTEN. Yes, because it was the language —
ALTA. Of their hearts.
RESTEN. There was no English in their hearts.
ALTA. No.
RESTEN. Consequently there is no English in our hearts.
ALTA. So true.
RESTEN. And that is why we can argue in it. Say mean, hateful, ugly thing — this is what English is perfect for!
ALTA. Yes. Make sense. See?
GEORGE. No, no make sense, I *don't* see.
ALTA. Mmm.
RESTEN. He is angry we are angry at each other.
GEORGE. I'm not angry, I'm — The whole point of having you here is to study — to record — your native tongue —

ALTA. Well, if he would apologize, then we could speak it.
RESTEN. Me apologize?!
ALTA. Yes. First time we are in plane, and you take the window — I can't see nothing! But this isn't so bad, okay, fine, you take window. No big shirt off my back. But then I have big thought —
RESTEN. Oh no —
ALTA. Oh yes! And big thought say: This is not just about plane ride, not just about armrest, no, this is about much bigger fish. This is what my husband is like, not just on plane but *in life.* In life, we are on plane, we are on journey, and always, ALWAYS he take the window seat.
RESTEN. I gave you my youth! I gave you my blood! Look at me now, an old man with a weak, weak heart —
ALTA. And me? I have weak heart too! My heart it HURTS all the time, hurts because I married you and not Gary Siga when I had the chance!
RESTEN. Oh, Gary Siga, Gary Siga, Gary fucking SIGA!
ALTA. Yes — he is good to wife! He does not take window seat! He say, "Here, sweetieheart, you are love of mine, so please, take window seat, I take middle and sit next to smelly man."
RESTEN. Complain, all you DO! Do I complain?
ALTA. Complain about what?
RESTEN. Complain about your bitching bad cooking, unh?!
(Alta gasps.)
ALTA. My COOKING.
RESTEN. YES.
ALTA. What is wrong with my COOKING.
RESTEN. Force it down my gullet I do, because it is like SLUDGEY.
ALTA. You used to LOVE MY FOOD. I see you, way you smack it down!
RESTEN. Because I PRETEND.
ALTA. OHHHHHH — you ... MAN. You awful, terrible MAN.
RESTEN. *(Pretending.)* Oh yes, this chicken is very good, oh, Alta, thank you — *(He mimes vomiting. Alta lunges for Resten.)*
ALTA. I hate you, I hate you, I hate you!
GEORGE. Let's calm down —
ALTA. *(To George.)* Do you know what is like to labor each day to make a meal with your own hands only to have it spit out?

RESTEN. Poisoning me you are!
ALTA. Less painful to be shot in the head, my friend, less painful to be stab in the chest!
RESTEN. Stab in chest? Walk in park compare to your stew! Salt in everything, it's deliberate, when you know about my heart — !
ALTA. That is IT. You have push me too far! I didn't want to do it but you make me do it! *(She looks directly at Resten and then puts a hex on him.)*
RESTEN. Crazy woman, NO!
ALTA. Dead to me, into the silence — never to stop, NEVER. *(She spits.)*
RESTEN. Oh yes? *(He throws a hex on her.)* Dead to me, into the silence — everlasting void, EVER. *(He spits. They both stop and turn away.)*
GEORGE. What is going on? *(He looks at Emma who is just as bewildered as he is.)* Alta…? Resten…? *(Neither speaks. They sit in stony silence.)* Resten! Alta!
ALTA. Yes.
GEORGE. Why aren't you speaking?
ALTA. Of course I am speaking. *(Significantly.)* To you.
GEORGE. What does that mean — what about Resten? *(An elaborate pause.)*
ALTA. Who?
GEORGE. Staff meeting! *(Lights shift. Alta and Resten go out as Emma retrieves a large book. She sits down at the table with George and cracks it open.)*
EMMA. According to the research, what we witnessed was a ghost curse.
GEORGE. A ghost curse?
EMMA. Yes, apparently Ellowans believe that if a person behaves reprehensibly then the community can make that person an outcast by … *(She reads.)* "effectively excommunicating the offending person. He or she is no longer spoken to or acknowledged. This 'silent treatment' then relegates the offender to the status of a ghost, wiping out his or her existence in the normal, daily affairs of life." That's awful. It's just like my parents' marriage.
GEORGE. How do you reverse it?
EMMA. You can't. Apparently, it's for life. Once you do it, you can't take it back.
GEORGE. So you're saying they'll never talk to each other again?

EMMA. Well … in order for them to do so we would need the services of an Ellowan shaman and the last one died in 1949.
GEORGE. 1949?
EMMA. I'm very sorry, George. *(Beat.)*
GEORGE. This is the worst day of my life.
EMMA. George, don't you think that's a bit of an overstatement?
GEORGE. Not really. *(He is abject. Emma wants very, very much to rest her hand on his shoulder and console him in some way. But she doesn't. She starts heading towards the door. George reaches into his pocket for a small cloth to wipe his glasses with. A note falls out.)*
EMMA. George. I was going to step out for a bit, but perhaps I should stay? That is, if you wanted me to, I could … George? *(But George is looking at the note.)*
GEORGE. What was that?
EMMA. I said … I'll be back soon.
GEORGE. All right. *(Emma goes. George reads the note.)* "She likes to visit other marriages like a tourist, but like a tourist, she knows she'll never get inside. Other marriages remain as mysterious as clocks, whose pleasant faces hide gears she'll never understand. Is it comfort or woe that every clock, no matter how fine, eventually lags behind…?"

Scene 6

The lab.

George reads from a book.

GEORGE. "We pushed on into the wilderness, and there, between the gorge and the river, we discovered a heretofore unknown group of people. They call themselves, 'Ell-o-wa': River People, and they speak a lilting, melodic tongue, not unlike the rushing of water. Legend has it that their language was created long ago by the first man and woman, who fell in love upon seeing each other and then needed words for all they wanted to convey. What sounds, what stops, what motions of teeth and tongue: All were chosen for what sounded beautiful. This was their courtship, and it is said, when this language was first spoken, it sounded exactly like song." *(By now George is in the lab with Alta and Resten. George closes the book.)* The world this book describes is gone. Dead. Never to return. And this beautiful, wondrous tongue, fashioned mysteriously and inexplicably — over centuries, perhaps, millennia — is about to disappear. Forever. We are standing on the precipice, my friends; you are staring at it right now. You are all that stands between an entire world and oblivion. So. I ask you. Will you choose to remember? Or will you choose to forget? *(Beat.)*
ALTA. Please tell the person at the other end of the table that he need to shower because smell of his cheap cologne is making me truly nauseous.
RESTEN. And please tell the woman she should learn some grammar because one is nauseated not nauseous.
GEORGE. *(Underneath.)* Oh, for the love of God …
ALTA. Please tell the person at the other end of the table that he smell like a dead weasel that's been caught in a trap laid with raccoon guts for seven days.
RESTEN. And tell the woman, oh, you mean like the smell of your COOKING?

ALTA. THASS ENOUGH. *(Alta reaches into a bag and brings up a covered Tupperware. She sets it in front of George and opens the lid.)* I want you eat that.

GEORGE. What?

RESTEN. Don't eat it.

ALTA. I don't hear anything except a little fly buzzing, do you?

RESTEN. Don't eat it.

ALTA. I am thinking you must think I am very bad cook. This hurts my heart so much, these terrible lies about me. So. I give you food. You eat. You see.

RESTEN. Don't eat it.

ALTA. There is nothing repulsive-ish about it. No liver. No brain. Not the lovely lobe of ear. Or even the tasty colon. No. I keep to safe, happy parts.

GEORGE. That's very kind of you, Alta, but frankly, I'm just not very hungry —

ALTA. Not hungry?! NOT HUNGRY?! *(Alta breaks out into racking sobs.)*

GEORGE. Alta…?

ALTA. HE won't eat, YOU won't eat — why doesn't ALTA just kill herself, UNH?

GEORGE. I meant no disrespect, Alta, please —

ALTA. I am useless, worse than a sterile goat, a woman who cannot cook — my ancestors would SPIT ON ME. I am a SHAME, a FAILURE, a WRETCHED UDDER-LESS COW — *(Alta produces a fork, aims it at herself. George grabs her arm —)*

GEORGE. Alta, NO, Alta, LOOK. *(He leans forward. He smells the food. She stops crying. A strange smell reaches his nose, neither pleasant nor unpleasant.)* Mmm. Smells … rich. *(Alta looks at him with tear-stained eyes.)*

ALTA. Very good for you too.

RESTEN. Don't eat it.

ALTA. You're hungry … aren't you? *(George realizes he is a little hungry. Alta presses her advantage.)* Maybe someone else is happy with dollar menu at McDonald's, but big smart scientist like you with big busy brain need nourishment. Real food. Yes? *(She gives George the fork. George accepts it. Resten puts his hand on George's arm.)*

RESTEN. I'm telling you. *(George looks at Resten. George looks at Alta. Alta looks at him encouragingly. George dips in the fork and*

slowly brings it to his mouth. Suddenly, the door opens. Mary tentatively looks in.)
MARY. George? *(George stops, mid-bite.)*
ALTA. RESTEN.
BAKAH! HA!
GEORGE. Mary.
MARY. Is this a bad time?
GEORGE. No, please. Please. Come in. Ah. Alta. Resten. If you could? *(Alta gives Mary the stinkeye. She and Resten go out.)*
MARY. I'm sorry, I didn't mean to interrupt —
GEORGE. No, no trouble, I'm — *(With hope.)* You didn't go. *(With despair.)* Why are you dressed like that?
MARY. This is what I wear. When I travel. *(She looks around.)* I didn't mean to come this way. The cab driver wanted to take this route —
GEORGE. A cab? Why? I could've given you a ride.
MARY. That's very nice of you, George, but I don't think that's how this works. *(Pause.)* Anyway. I didn't realize we'd be going right by the campus. I found myself saying, "I need to make a stop" before I even knew I was going to say it.
GEORGE. And where exactly are you going?
MARY. To the station. And after that ... I'm not really sure. *(Beat.)* George, there's something I wanted to ask you ... about the way we left things ...
GEORGE. Yes...?
MARY. ... Are you sure you have nothing to say to me? *(George opens his mouth to speak. Mary waits, hopeful.)*
GEORGE. I ... I ...
MARY. You must have something to say. *(George struggles to speak. George struggles to speak. Mary turns to go.)*
GEORGE. Did you know that I can remember everything you wore on our first date? You wore a blue shirt that had part of a handprint on it. In white. *(Mary stops, listening.)*
MARY. *(A little surprised.)* It was flour; I'd been baking bread that day ...
GEORGE. ... And you smelled like bread. You wore jeans, those jeans you don't wear anymore —
MARY. I can't fit in them anymore ... all that bread ...
GEORGE. ... And a belt that had stripes on it like a rainbow. And black shoes with a very square toe; I remember looking at them and

thinking they looked witch-like but in a good way, a cute way.
MARY. A cute witch way?
GEORGE. Yes. And I liked your knees because they turned in a bit to look at each other and I thought these are the knees of a woman I could love.
MARY. Yes?
GEORGE. Yes.
MARY. George.
GEORGE. Mary. *(They recognize each other. Mary starts to move towards him.)*
MARY. And?
GEORGE. And?
MARY. Oh. There is no and?
GEORGE. I just told you I loved you —
MARY. That's not exactly what you said —
GEORGE. Then just tell me what you want and I'll say it!
MARY. Oh, George, that's not how it works —
GEORGE. STOP SAYING THAT. Stop saying *you* know how it works and *I* don't, like this is some kind of *process* that has pre-ordained *rules* and why can't you just admit it, you *did* write those notes, YOU DID. *(She just looks at him.)*
MARY. This was. Clearly this was …
GEORGE. You came just to leave again? Why? Why?
MARY. I'm sorry, George. I really am. I — *(She goes. George falls to the ground.)*

Scene 7

An office. Emma and the instructor sit at a table.

The instructor is an older German woman with angular glasses, spiky short hair and very red, rosy cheeks. She's very encouraging, very earnest with only the slightest German accent.

INSTRUCTOR. Again.
EMMA. Keel vi numi … ĝes?
INSTRUCTOR. *(Correcting.)* Kiel vi *no*miĝas!
EMMA. Sorry. Kiel vi *no*miĝas. Min nom …
INSTRUCTOR. Min nomiĝ*as* Emma.
EMMA. Min nomiĝes — *ĝas* — Emma —
INSTRUCTOR. Good!
EMMA. No, it's not, it's not good at all —
INSTRUCTOR. You are getting the hang of it, do not despair!
EMMA. I sound — silly. All clunky and harsh and —
INSTRUCTOR. No, no, no, you must not say that. Esperanto is the most beautiful language in the world. You just don't know it yet.
EMMA. I just don't seem to be very good at it; I know it's a very logical language, but I can't seem to —
INSTRUCTOR. Anyone can learn Esperanto. If you are not learning it, I must be doing something wrong, yes it must be me —
EMMA. No, that's not what I —
INSTRUCTOR. I must be teaching you wrong, because I am awful, yes, the worst, most terrible teacher of Esperanto in all the world —
EMMA. I wouldn't say that, really. I'm just not very good at languages, at least not the live ones —
INSTRUCTOR. No, no. Zamenhof, God rest his soul, made a language anyone could learn. Millions of people have learned it with ease and alacrity. If you are not learning it, then it must be my failure —
EMMA. Please, I really wish you wouldn't take it so personally.

INSTRUCTOR. How can I not? Zamenhof would be ashamed, yes, so ashamed ... unless ... unless it is not me, but ... you.
EMMA. Me?
INSTRUCTOR. Yes, you. Perhaps you have some kind of block? Some kind of pih-sychological reason to not want to learn the most perfect, beautiful language in the world?
EMMA. Uh ...
INSTRUCTOR. Some kind of traüma? Some kind of stress? Why do you want to learn this language?
EMMA. Why?
INSTRUCTOR. Yes, why? What is the reason make you call me? Make you come here? Make you try to learn Esperanto?
EMMA. Well ... I ... I've always liked the idea of Esperanto. You know, the idea of a universal language ... and Zamenhof, I mean, his story is so inspiring, how he hoped for peace and understanding —
INSTRUCTOR. Yes, yes, this is all common, but something special? Something more?
EMMA. I'm afraid I don't see what you mean ...
INSTRUCTOR. Okay, let me spell it out. El-Oh-Fee-Ee.
EMMA. Elloffee?
INSTRUCTOR. LOVE! All second languages are learned out of love! Oh yes. Woman love Italian culture, love Italian food, Italian way of life — bam! That is why she learn Italian! People world all over love American movie, love American TV — bam! That is why they all learn English! Always love, love, love. So what do you love?
EMMA. What do I?
INSTRUCTOR. What do you love that make you learn Esperanto?
EMMA. I ... I'm not sure I follow ...
INSTRUCTOR. I knew a Dutch girl once — you know the Dutch? They speak languages like cauliflowers!
EMMA. Okay, I don't know what that means.
INSTRUCTOR. They are coming out of their ears! This makes the Dutch very smug. Very insufferable. And this girl, she broke my heart. But that is another story. Thing about this girl was she *had* to learn languages. She was compelled. Each new language was like unlocking a door to a vast and otherwise impenetrable landscape. And once she started, she could not stop. So now. If you cannot learn a tongue, what does this mean? Is it not possible that the *opposite* is true? That if you find you are blocked — resistant — this

could mean you do *not* want to open that door? That perhaps, you are afraid of what might be on the other side?
EMMA. Afraid?
INSTRUCTOR. It is a scary thing to speak and be entendu. Comprende?
EMMA. Yes, … I think so.
INSTRUCTOR. Then go. Think on it. You must ask yourself: what am I afraid of? Who am I afraid to know?
EMMA. Who am I afraid to know.
INSTRUCTOR. Yes. Only then will you be able to call yourself by the name: Esperantisto!
EMMA. I'll try.
INSTRUCTOR. You will. *(Emma starts putting on her coat.)*
EMMA. I never knew speaking a language required such … bravery.
INSTRUCTOR. My dear. Nothing on earth could possibly require more. *(Emma goes.)*

Scene 8

George.

GEORGE. I lie on the floor of the lab. For how long, I don't know. But I have a kind of waking dream. I dream the floor of the lab has become a boneyard of language. Scraps of words and languages lying in heaps everywhere. Over here, lying on its back, is "Ohrwurm," German for "ear worm," a song that you can't get out of your head. And over there, is "ambisinistrous," being left-handed in both hands. By my feet: "lethologica," the inability to recall the right word. And there, right in front of me, are all the words I should've said to Mary, but didn't — *(Mary appears at a remove.)*
MARY. Say the right thing, George. Say the right thing and maybe I won't go. Maybe this isn't all irretrievably broken. Maybe we can still go on to have a life together, maybe even grow a little old together and die in that non-tragic way you're so fond of. So. What do you have to say for yourself? *(The door opens. Alta and Resten enter. Mary disappears.)*

ALTA. And when I get home, I will be calling wonderful Gary Siga and saying, hey, Gary, how is your wife? / How is Taji? Is she happy? Of course she happy! She has wonderful husband! Nicest husband in four villages!

RESTEN. And when I get home, I will be going to Ahvia's restaurant, yes, because everyone know she make best-best goat stew, oh! NO ONE make goat stew like Ahvia!

ALTA. *(Overlapping.)* AHVIA IS A BAKAH-HOLE AND EVERYONE KNOWING THAT!

RESTEN. *(Overlapping.)* Ambrosia, Ahvia's stew! *(Alta takes out the Tupperware container and tears off the lid.)*

ALTA. Ahvia couldn't cook a stew this good if SHE COOK A THOUSAND YEARS! *(Resten grabs the Tupperware.)*

RESTEN. Someone close it! Stench make Resten want to THROW UP and DIE —

ALTA. THEN DIE! *(Alta lunges for the Tupperware, raining blows down on Resten.)*

ALTA. Goddamn FUCK-BUTT, no-good shit SHIT SHIT —	RESTEN. DON'T FEEL NOTHING! I DON'T SEE NO ONE — !

GEORGE. STOP IT! *(Alta and Resten are stunned by the ferocity of George's cry. Words cannot adequately describe George's cry. It's primal. It's a wail. Its sheer force makes the walls shudder.)* What is WRONG with you?! You two are acting like CHILDREN and I am sick of it, do you hear me, SICK of it! And if you don't resolve this, I'm going to send you right back to where you came from, where you two can torture yourselves as much as you like for the rest of your pathetic, miserable lives! I mean, MY GOD. You two could have had it all, it was right within your grasp! But through sheer selfishness and pig-headedness and meanness, you've chosen darkness, you've chosen isolation, you've chosen loss. You're letting your whole world slip through your fingers. All of it is disappearing and you won't even — you won't FIGHT for it, fight for its existence. And excuse me if that makes me CRAZY, excuse me if I find that just unbelievably WRONG. *(Beat. Alta and Resten do not talk to each other but they do talk somewhat towards each other.)*

ALTA. Sound like Mister Science Man is a bit upset.

RESTEN. Maybe because his wife left him.

GEORGE. What?

ALTA. Very sad when marriage not work out. Quite a pickle.

GEORGE. How...?
ALTA. Walls are thin.
RESTEN. Practically nonexistent.
ALTA. No need for secrets, Mister Science Man. We are your friend.
GEORGE. It's temporary, a temporary — We are taking time off. That's it, okay? That's all.
RESTEN. Time off? Sound more like goodbye.
ALTA. Good bye.
RESTEN. Didn't you hear it?
ALTA. How could you not hear it?
RESTEN. I can't even hear out my left ear and I heard it.
GEORGE. You're both — you don't know what you're talking about.
ALTA. Okay, Mister Science Man.
GEORGE. That's enough for today. *(George moves towards the door.)*
ALTA. George. Maybe you not understanding something. You think loss of our language is loss of our world. And is okay you think that; you are linguist; you think everything is about language. But it is world that ends first, my friend. World die and then language follow. Our world is already gone. And what we accept, which maybe you do not, is: no amount of talk talk talk will ever bring what is gone back. *(George looks at Alta. And then, he goes.)*

Scene 9

The lab.

Alta and Resten sit in silence. They do not look at each other.

The silence lengthens.

Finally, Alta clears her throat.

Beat.

ALTA. Sad. So sad. To be so young. And left alone. *(They continue to look straight ahead, no eye contact.)*
RESTEN. *(Quietly.)* Viremte mat Gary Siga shushte? *[Do you really wish you'd married Gary Siga?]* *(Their language is indeed beautiful. It may very well be the most beautiful language ever heard. It is like song.)*
ALTA. Erfullah soenne. Mir loftsi usjut? *(Dismissively.)* Gary Siga. *[We're all old. What does it matter? Gary Siga.]* *(She shrugs.)*
RESTEN. Mir ne glessalla. *[Don't leave me.]* *(Alta reaches out and puts her hand on his. They finally look at each other.)*
ALTA. Istulla meh. *[I won't.]* *(A moment as they squeeze hands. And then Alta, without breaking off her gaze with Resten, reaches over and produces another container of food and a fork from her bag. She beams at Resten as she takes off the lid. Resten gamely smiles back. But his lips quiver. Alta pushes the food and the fork into Resten's hands. Resten slowly digs out a bit of food. Alta watches him like a mother watching her baby about to eat solid food for the first time. But now, Resten seems to waver and Alta starts to notice. The nausea is almost overwhelming him now. The fork trembles. His hand trembles. Sweat is pouring off him. Alta's eyes get bigger and bigger as the fork comes closer and closer ...)*
RESTEN. NO, I can't, I can't! *(He pushes away the food and starts to retch, then grimace in pain. Alta's hurt immediately turns to concern.)*
ALTA. Resten? *(Resten doubles over.)* Resten! Ellessa? Ellessa! *(Resten suddenly gives a loud, sharp exhale. The lights go out, as if he's*

blown them out. Beat. A railway platform appears. Mary walks on, holding her suitcase. She glances at a train schedule. She walks along the edge of the platform and cranes her neck to look one way down the track and then the other.)

Scene 10

The train station.

Mary stands by the tracks. She notices her hands and takes off her ring. She walks to the edge of the platform and stares at the tracks. And then she puts her ring back on and sits down, twisting it absentmindedly.

An old man enters, holding a box. It is wrapped in brown paper and tied up with string.

OLD MAN. Excuse me, excuse me, do you have the time?
MARY. Yes, it's — you're wearing a watch.
OLD MAN. Oh, I know, but you see I'm always worried that my watch is a little fast or a little slow — it's an old watch, very valuable, sentimentally speaking — and so I have to ask people constantly what time it is to check it and make sure it's accurate.
MARY. That seems, if you don't mind me saying, to completely defeat the purpose of wearing a watch.
OLD MAN. Indeed, indeed. Are you considering throwing it on the tracks?
MARY. What?
OLD MAN. Your ring. I couldn't help but notice the way you've been twisting it, as if you're doubting whether you should stay married at all, wondering if it all wasn't an error, a delusion, a dream.
MARY. For your information, I was simply noticing how dirty it was and thinking to myself I needed to clean it.
OLD MAN. My mistake, my mistake.
MARY. I find making those kinds of assumptions fairly rude.
OLD MAN. I am rude. It is because I am old.

MARY. Well that's no excuse.
OLD MAN. You'll be rude too when you're old. You'll see.
MARY. I don't think so.
OLD MAN. So you left.
MARY. Excuse me?
OLD MAN. Your husband.
MARY. How did you know?
OLD MAN. Your suitcase. Your clothes. Your air of guilt and freedom. And where do you plan to go?
MARY. I don't know.
OLD MAN. I see.
MARY. Not that it's any of your concern.
OLD MAN. It certainly isn't, I agree. *(Pause.)* Might I inquire, though … why?
MARY. Why?
OLD MAN. Why did you leave? It seems to me, if you don't mind my saying, like a fairly large decision. And most of us, let us face it, do all we can *not* to change. But here you are: a woman who has chosen change. And so I am curious. Why?
MARY. Because. Because. I don't really know. I'm sorry.
OLD MAN. You don't have to apologize, my dear. That is a good answer.
MARY. It's not … ridiculous?
OLD MAN. No. It is very hard to know what we know. People can spend a life trying to figure out such a thing. Do you know what you plan to do?
MARY. No. To be honest. I have no idea.
OLD MAN. So. Here we are. Two travelers. A woman who has embarked on a new life. And a man who is contemplating ending his.
MARY. Excuse me?
OLD MAN. My plan today is to jump in front of the next train.
MARY. You must be — that's not true.
OLD MAN. Oh, but it is true.
MARY. No it isn't. You're not really going to do that.
OLD MAN. Oh yes. Quite really.
MARY. But why?
OLD MAN. I don't know.
MARY. Are you sad?
OLD MAN. No.
MARY. Then why?

OLD MAN. I woke up this morning and felt like life was devoid of any meaning.
MARY. I too have felt that way. Many times.
OLD MAN. I felt that nothing I did would ever have much significance in the world —
MARY. Yes, me too —
OLD MAN. And that every day was just a trudging forth, a monotonous sameness, one foot in front of the other, but for what?
MARY. Yes, exactly. For what?
OLD MAN. But you see I do not have it as easy as you. I have no state I can change so easily. Nothing to blame for my lack of meaning except myself. I have no children. I have no wife. I have no work — not anymore.
MARY. But that's ... wonderful.
OLD MAN. To have nothing?
MARY. To have nothing. To be tied to nothing. To be your own. I think that's both the saddest thing I've ever heard and the most wonderful. *(Pause.)* Maybe you could go a little further into your sadness. And see what's there. Can you?
OLD MAN. I don't know ...
MARY. It's like this: It's like you're in a room. And you think it's the very last room. But there's another, even further. There's a door. Can you see it? Can you open it? *(The Old Man closes his eyes.)*
OLD MAN. I might ...
MARY. Do you know, how when you close your eyes tight and can see nothing — it's only then that there are sparks of light?
OLD MAN. A door ...
MARY. Go into that sadness further ... and then maybe ...
OLD MAN. There can be light.
MARY. A kind of light. *(The distant sound of an oncoming train.)* All I know is sometimes you can feel so sad, it begins to feel like happiness. And you can be so happy that it starts to feel like grief. You can feel so alive, it starts to feel like death. And you can feel so dead that you start to feel alive. And some people — most people — live their whole lives without touching any of these places at all. But I do. And you might. *(The sound of the oncoming train grows louder. The train passes. It is a rushing, deafening sound. Wind sweeps across the platform. But Mary and the Old Man are still. The train is gone. Silence.)* Did you see it? The door? The other room?
OLD MAN. Not quite yet. But I might.

MARY. I'm glad you didn't jump.
OLD MAN. I don't know why I didn't. I might tomorrow. *(Pause.)* I'm glad you didn't throw your ring on the tracks. *(Mary looks at her hand.)*
MARY. I don't know why I didn't. I might tomorrow. *(She takes her ring off and looks at it. She slips it into her pocket.)* I'm hungry.
OLD MAN. Famished.
MARY. We should eat something.
OLD MAN. Perhaps ... you'd like to join me?
MARY. Actually ... I would. *(He offers her his arm. She takes it. They start to walk off.)* Not to be nosy, but what is in that box?
OLD MAN. Well, my dear, now that is a long story ... *(They go. George quickly walks onto the platform. He glances at a train schedule. He walks along the edge of the platform and cranes his neck to look one way down the track and then the other.)*

Scene 11

George's house. He is haunted by regret.

GEORGE. Should I have vacuumed the stairs? Carved the roast? Hung the pictures? Should I have mowed the lawn, planted a lawn, put up some bookshelves? Yes? No? How does this work? *(George takes the cushions out of the chairs and sofa. He flips through all the books. He lifts up the rug. He moves aside knick-knacks, searching. Every careful thing is undone.)* Should I have bought the coat, waxed the car, fixed the faucet, learned how to season a skillet? Or none? Or more? At all? *(He finds a bottle of Scotch.)* Well. How now brown cow. *(He toasts.)* To my wife, Mary. Who left me. Twice. And it's like I can still hear her voice, saying: George, I can hear you. I'm right here, she says. I'm right here. *(There's no one there. He drinks. He is weary. And then he has a thought. He goes to his slippers, looks inside. Mary's last note falls out. George is about to unfold it, then stops. He puts it, unread, into his breast pocket and then puts his hand there. He holds it there for some time.)*

Scene 12

The hospital.

Resten is in bed. Alta is next to him. As she talks, Emma enters and stands in the doorway, listening.

ALTA. Resten — Resten, luende. Rella soesse, mir oona fes ayanna parta. Shuss, liante, mak needah. Bameh nir "fuck-butt" ustorelleh. Nir mandeh obria. Nir possen ulivitia. An mir ne glessalla. Ohneegeh mar vi os? Lassella mani oh bessella mi onde ahvi rossa? *[Resten — Resten, listen to me. If you stay, I promise I'll be nice to you. Kind, generous, every day of your life. I won't call you a fuck-butt anymore. I won't hit you on the head. I won't jab you in the ribs. Just don't leave me. What will I do if you go? How will I remember all that I'm supposed to know?] (Hopeful.)* Resten? *(Soft.)* Resten. *(No response. Quietly.)* Mir ne glessalla. *(Beat.)*
EMMA. How is he?
ALTA. Eh.
EMMA. I just spoke to the doctor. Alta. Resten's very ill. He's been ill for a long time. That's why he lost his appetite.
ALTA. That's why he is not eating?
EMMA. Yes.
ALTA. Not because he not love me?
EMMA. No.
ALTA. Well. Well. *(She dabs at her eyes with the corner of her dress.)* Why he not tell me, stupid man? *(Pause.)* When will he get better? How long?
EMMA. That's the thing, Alta. No one knows. What he has ... they say it can't be cured. I'm so, so sorry. *(Alta adjusts Resten's covers.)*
ALTA. Well. We are old. Not a lot of time anyway.
EMMA. Alta? Could I ask you something? I heard you talking to him. I thought the Ghost Curse ... I thought it was permanent.
ALTA. It is.
EMMA. Then how...?
ALTA. Real Ghost Curse takes four dead animals, a shaman and a

very long pipe. We sort of do bastard ghost curse, English-style. If it were in Elloway then once we do it, can never take back. But say something in English and everyone know you don't really mean it. Say it in English and you can always take it back.
EMMA. Are there words in Elloway that have no equivalent in English?
ALTA. Yeah, like whole thing! Whole thing have no equivalent.
EMMA. But specific words for specific things.
ALTA. Take pick! In Elloway, we never say time move forward or backward. Time is like pool of water, big or small. When day is slow we have big time. When we are rush, we have small time. There is word for kind of woman who is beautiful when you see her from far away but not so beautiful when you see her up close. There is word for man who act younger and younger as he gets older and older. All sort of useful word with no English version.
EMMA. How do you say, "I love you," in Elloway?
ALTA. We don't say it like that, like something you feel. We say, Mir Ne Glessalla.
EMMA. Mir. Ne. Glessalla.
ALTA. Mir ne glessalla. Which literally mean: Don't leave me. Because that is what "I love you" mean to us. *(Looking at Resten.)* I never want to be left by you. I never want you not with me.
EMMA. Mir ne glessalla.
ALTA. Maybe you should tell it to your Mr. Science Man. See what happen.
EMMA. Why would I do that? *(Alta looks at Emma. A moment.)*
ALTA. No reason. Anyway, is just an idea. Everyone need someone to say hello to in the morning and goodbye to at night.
EMMA. I don't know if it's that easy.
ALTA. True. Lotta men are kinda thick. Resten, I had to chase him for year before he finally say yes.
EMMA. I thought you were the one being chased. By Gary Siga.
ALTA. Oh no. I never want Gary Siga. But after year of chasing Resten, he still running round with this girl, that girl. Rana Mossi. Fifi Gogot. Very annoying. Resten, think he is some big gift from God. So then I go out with Gary Siga. To make Resten jealous. But I never want Gary. I only want Resten. Tell you truth, I only ever want Resten. Nobody else.
RESTEN. *(Very faintly and without opening his eyes.)* Ha. *(Alta gasps.)*
ALTA. Resten! You awake!

RESTEN. Oh yes.
ALTA. For your information, buddy, I only say what I say to make you feel better.
RESTEN. Hee hee.
ALTA. Oh, I hate you. You are a terrible man.
RESTEN. Yeah yeah, come kiss this terrible man. *(Alta kisses Resten. Emma quietly leaves as Alta and Resten begin what can only be described as a heavy-duty make-out session.)*

Scene 13

George's house.

George is lying on the floor.

There's a knock at the door.

EMMA. *(Offstage.)* George? George. *(Emma tentatively opens the door and enters.)* George? *(She realizes he's asleep. She sees the bottle of Scotch next to him and the glass. Surprised and a little disapproving.)* George. *(She goes to wake him and then stops. He looks as if he could use the rest. She looks around, curious.)* So this is your house. *(She runs her hand over his books.)* Your books. *(She picks up a photo frame.)* Your wife. *(To the photo.)* Hello, George's wife. Have a seat? Why thank you, George. I don't mind if I do. *(She sits and regards George.)* You know, George ... you look especially handsome today in that shirt that doesn't match your eyes. You haven't worn it in a while and I'm glad to see it reappear. I have fond associations of it. You wore it when we went to that conference in Atlanta and we had lunch at the Au Bon Pain and you complained about how Americans pronounce, "Au Bon Pain," which is pretty much how I pronounce, "Au Bon Pain," and so I just kept quiet. We had cream of broccoli soup. George. You know, sometimes? There's a little bit of hair sticking up at the back of your head and it makes me sad. As does the sound of your voice, and the way, sometimes, the elastic on your socks gives out and I can see them slumping around your ankles. In Ubykh, "you please me" translates literally to "you cut my heart." George. You cut my heart. *(Slowly, as if she can't quite help herself, she reaches out to touch him. George stirs. She quickly withdraws her hand.)* George? *(George sits up. He looks at Emma. He is confused.)* Hello.

GEORGE. Is this a dream?

EMMA. No.

GEORGE. Are you sure?

EMMA. Yes.

GEORGE. *(Disappointed.)* Oh.

EMMA. George, I've been looking for you everywhere. I called and called.

GEORGE. I was at the train station. Then the bus station. It seemed like there were women with suitcases everywhere.

EMMA. George, listen. I need you to come with me.

GEORGE. Why? Where?

EMMA. It's a long story. I'll explain on the way. *(She helps him to his feet.)* They're talking again.

GEORGE. They are? They are. *(And even though he doesn't say it, this is what he is thinking: "Even their marriage is better than mine.")*

EMMA. Come on. *(She helps him with his jacket. He runs his hands through his hair.)*

GEORGE. How do I look? *(Emma takes him in. She clearly thinks he looks wonderful.)*

EMMA. Fine.

Scene 14

The hospital.

Resten's room. Resten is lying on the bed, trying to turn on the TV with the remote control.

George walks in.

RESTEN. Hey. Mr. Science Man. Come in. Have seat.
GEORGE. What happened?
RESTEN. Oh, nothing to worry about.
GEORGE. Resten ...
RESTEN. It's true. Good thing about life is it is full of nasty surprises, but death, when you are old, is not one of them.
GEORGE. Well, I'm sorry, Resten. I really am.
RESTEN. Why? Not your fault. And maybe is better I'm here. You know, medicine not so good in our village. Here all fancy. Beep beep here, boop boop there.
GEORGE. Is Alta okay?
RESTEN. She wanted to go and cook something. Bring me food. That woman, if she could strap an oven to her back, she would. But what is happening with you? Your wife. She is really gone? *(George doesn't know what to say. Resten sighs.)* Very hard. This marriage business. Ellowans used to have up to three wives. But then three wives such pain in the ass, husbands beg to have it go down to just one.
GEORGE. She was so unhappy. But when we first met ... when we first met. God. You should have seen her. She was something. She really was. *(Beat.)*
RESTEN. Lemme tell you story. In the beginning of the world, there was a warrior. Big, handsome, strong kind of guy. And he have to go off and capture the golden fleek.
GEORGE. Fleece?
RESTEN. No, fleek, whatsa fleece? Fleek is kind of bird. Anyway. Fleek has nest at the top of highest tree in all of world. So warrior, say we call him, Resten, he has to climb this tree. And we are

talking one big fucking tree. But this bird, let us call her, Alta, she is very crafty. She like to play, "Hey, come get me if you can, nyah nyah nyah." So. What can Resten do? He have to climb fucking tree. So he climb and climb and finally he get to top of tree. And he grab Alta by the ankle so she cannot fly away. Alta, she is — holy cow — she is flip out! She is panic! She does not want to get caught! And Resten did not know this, but Alta, she is a changer! Suddenly, she become a tiger! And roar! And Resten, he is thinking, holy shit! But he do not let go. Then she become a gorilla and oh, this is very scary, she is roaring in his face, like to try to eat him. But he hold on, hold on. And then she change again, and this time, motherfucker, she is scariest thing EVER in whole world! She is demon and hairy monster and white man with gun all roll up in one! And Resten, he just about want to soil himself he is so scared! But he do not let go! He grip tighter and tighter the scareder and scareder he get! And then: You know what happen? The bird, she change into one last form and this is her true form. And you know what it is? A little lamb. Nothing but a little lamb. Meek and mild and beautiful. That's all she really was the whole time. She only become all those terrible things because she was scare. That is marriage, my friend. Same as myth. Except, each is both hunter and changer. Do you understand? Each grabs ankle of the other. Each is terrified of the other. And each take on many, many different form. But you hold on. Because if you hold on no matter how scare you get, something amazing happen: Everyone become too tired to change. And we become who we really are. No more roar, no more fang, no more claw — No. We are two lambs. We are two sparrows. We are mild and meek. And you know what else?

GEORGE. Beautiful?

RESTEN. Beautiful. *(Resten closes his eyes with a smile.)*

GEORGE. ... Resten?

RESTEN. Sleep ... maybe ... just for a little while ...

GEORGE. *(To himself, to the air.)* But she let go, Resten. She let go. *(And then, something strange happens. A profound sadness washes over George. It's like nothing he's ever felt before.)* Oh. God. *(He is overwhelmed with grief.)* Is this how it feels? *(He is overwhelmed with grief.)* This is how it feels. *(Emma enters.)*

EMMA. How's he doing? George, are you — *(The words die on her lips when she sees George's face.)* ... George...?

GEORGE. She left.

EMMA. ... What?
GEORGE. My wife. Left. *(What happens next stuns her. Very, very slowly and very, very gently, he embraces her. As she holds him, Emma is overcome with joy. As he is held, George is overcome with sadness. And when they embrace, it is the embrace of perfect happiness and perfect sadness. They stand there like that for a long, long moment.)*

End of Act One

ACT TWO

Scene 1

The lab. A wall of shelves. George goes up and down a ladder that rolls, retrieving tapes.

GEORGE. A short lesson in Esperanto. Mi estas amata. *(He looks at the audience.)* Mi estas amata. *(He waits until the audience responds.)* I am being loved. *(From here on out, after every colon, he will wait for the audience's response as he continues gathering tapes.)* Mi estas amita: I have been loved. Mi estas amota: I am about to be loved. Mi estis amata: I was loved. Mi estis amita: I had been loved. Mi estis amota: I was about to be loved.

Scene 2

An office.

INSTRUCTOR. Kiom kostas la kuko? *[How much is the cake?]* Kiom kostas la kuko? ... Emma? Cu vi kompren/is? *[Did you understand?]*
EMMA. I love George. *(She covers her face.)*
INSTRUCTOR. Nu! Kiu estas George? *[Well! Who is George?]*
EMMA. He's. The most wonderful. He's my boss.
INSTRUCTOR. Kaj vi estas enamiĝinta? *[And you're in love?]*
EMMA. Yes — absolutely, completely, terribly in love!
INSTRUCTOR. Depost kiam? *[Since when?]*
EMMA. I'm not sure. At first, I thought it was only recent, but the more I think about it, the clearer it is that I've been in love with him the entire time I've known him — four, maybe five years —
INSTRUCTOR. KVAR AŬ KVIN JAROJ?! *[FOUR OR FIVE YEARS?!]*

EMMA. Yes.
INSTRUCTOR. Kaj vi neniam diris? *[And you never SAID IT?]*
EMMA. I couldn't — he was married.
INSTRUCTOR. Ah.
EMMA. Oh my goodness. I can't believe I've actually told someone!
INSTRUCTOR. Okay, jen kion vi devas fari: *[Okay, here's what you must do:]* Vi devas diri al li. *[You must say it to him.]*
EMMA. Tell him? I couldn't!
INSTRUCTOR. Vi devas! *[You must!]*
EMMA. In Esperanto?
INSTRUCTOR. No, in English, in whatever language you are most comfortable with!
EMMA. But he doesn't — I mean, I'm pretty sure if he were going to fall in love with me he would've done it by now —
INSTRUCTOR. Does not matter! You must get it off your chest, get it off your mind. This is the only way! Until you do, Esperanto will not enter you! You have too much fear, too much doubt, too much *angst*.
EMMA. But I don't think I can.
INSTRUCTOR. Okay, then: second story of the Dutch girl.
EMMA. The one who broke your heart?
INSTRUCTOR. None other! She was beautiful this Dutch girl: six feet tall and built like a Viking! She could swim in frozen rivers, catch rabbits with her bare hands. She taught me how to cook a fish and build a kleedhokie. Oh, I was in love and everywhere it was summer!
EMMA. And then?
INSTRUCTOR. And then came The Basque Man.
EMMA. The Basque Man?
INSTRUCTOR. Yes! The Basque Man with his beret set at a rakish angle.
EMMA. What happened?
INSTRUCTOR. Is it not obvious? I, who had only ever known German, was no match for the romance and mystery of the Basque Man. It was a new door and though I did all I could to keep her, she was already fumbling for the keys!
EMMA. So what did you do?
INSTRUCTOR. What could I do? I told her I loved her! I told her I could not live without her! I told her the sun rose on this shoulder and set on the other!

EMMA. And?

INSTRUCTOR. And then she left.

EMMA. Didn't she understand you?

INSTRUCTOR. Are you not listening? She was Dutch! She spoke better German than I!

EMMA. Then I don't understand —

INSTRUCTOR. Don't you see? Yes, I was heartbroken, but while I was in love with her, I was too afraid to learn a single tongue — she was a master speaker, how could I let her see my inadequacies? But in professing my love for her, something inside me loosened. She was gone, yes — but she left the door open! That is why you must tell him. Not for him — never for him — for yourself! This is your greatest fear and you must face it! Yes, it might break you to do so, but if you don't, how else will you ever be free?

EMMA. But what if I don't have it in me...?

INSTRUCTOR. You do! YOU MUST! Love makes warriors of us all. Homoj kiel mi ne konas timon! Men such as me know no fear! Say it! Homoj kiel mi ne konas timon!

EMMA. *(Struggling through it.)* Homoj kiel mi ne konas timon.

INSTRUCTOR. HOMOJ KIEL MI NE KONAS TIMON!

EMMA. HOMOJ KIEL MI NE KONAS TIMON!

TOGETHER. HOMOJ KIEL MI NE KONAS TIMON!

INSTRUCTOR. Now go out there and say, George, I love you!

EMMA. George I love you!

INSTRUCTOR. GEORGE I LOVE YOU!

EMMA. GEORGE I LOVE YOU!

INSTRUCTOR. GEORGE MI AMAS VIN!

EMMA. George MI AMAS VIN!

TOGETHER. GEORGE MI AMAS VIN! *(Emma walks back to the lab all fired up.)*

EMMA. I leave the office and I feel GREAT. I feel like I'm on top of the world! I'm going to walk into the lab and tell George how I feel! Fear be damned! I can't wait! And suddenly, I realize it's a beautiful day. People pass by and my God — they're beautiful! They're gorgeous! Why haven't I seen it before? People pass by. The women are beautiful. Their babies are beautiful. Even the beggars are beautiful. And then — suddenly — a breeze lifts across my face and brings with it — *(She takes a very deep inhale. The theater is flooded, and I mean absolutely flooded, by the most amazing smell. She stops a passerby.)* Excuse me, excuse me — but what in the world is

that incredible smell?
PASSERBY. It is the smell of bread.
EMMA. But where is it coming from? *(The passerby points.)*
PASSERBY. There.
EMMA. I follow his hand and see: The Blue Tulip Bakeshop. The sunlight hits it at a slant and it looks so perfect, so beautiful that it looks just like a movie set, someone's perfect idea of what a bakery should look like. Except it's real, it's right there. And it's like those cartoons, you know, where the scent of food becomes a hand and the fingers of the hand lift a character by the nose, right out of his seat. That's what I feel happening to me. *(Emma enters the bakery. A little bell tinkles. Emma almost swoons from the heavenly aroma.)* And in the back, I see the most beautiful woman I have ever seen in my life. *(A woman is there, baking. She is radiant. She kneads dough. She is wonderful.)*
WOMAN. *(Laughing.)* Welcome! Welcome. You don't know it yet, but you are the luckiest person in the world.
EMMA. Why?
WOMAN. Because this is just out of the oven. *(She hands Emma a piece of bread. Emma hesitates.)* Hurry — it won't be the same if it cools! *(Emma eats the bread. She closes her eyes.)*
EMMA. Oh ... it's so ... good ... *(She opens her eyes. And suddenly she realizes who the woman is.)* Mary? *(Mary looks at her with friendly, curious eyes.)*
MARY. Do I know you?
EMMA. I'm ... I'm ... No, I must be mistaken. I thought you were a different Mary.
MARY. A different Mary! How marvelous. I've never been mistaken for another Mary before. What can I do for you?
EMMA. I was walking by and then I smelled your bread ...
MARY. We have sourdough, of course, but also lavender-chocolate, four-grain lemon-pomegranate, wild honey and pistachio, fig and manchego —
EMMA. And do you make them all yourself?
MARY. I make them all myself. I bake bread all through the night. And when the bread is all gone, I close the shop and then I go home and sleep. Sometimes I dream I'm baking bread and that is how it goes, from a waking happiness to a sleeping happiness and back. Like water being poured back and forth between two cups. *(She laughs as she talks and it really is the most enchanting sound.)*

EMMA. You're that happy?
MARY. Oh yes. Happiest I've ever been in my entire life.
EMMA. How did you come to do this?
MARY. Well, quite recently, I left my husband. *(A shadow crosses her face, briefly.)* That was a hard time.
EMMA. Why did you leave?
MARY. Well, it sounds strange to say it, but the truth was, I was sad. I'd simply become too sad to stay. So I left. I left without much. Just a suitcase. And I really didn't have a plan. And then, I was at the train station, wondering where I should go. And there was an old man there. He asked me for the time and we started talking. He told me he was a baker but that he was leaving his bakery. Why, I asked him. He told me he was tired of baking bread. He had never wanted to be a baker. But his father had been a baker and his father's father had been a baker and so on and so forth — his last name was actually "Baker" if you can believe it. Anyway, this man told me he'd decided enough was enough. He locked up his bakery, put up a sign that said, "Closed until further notice," and he was off. Then I noticed he was carrying a very odd box and I've always been the curious type so I asked him what was in it. And he sighed a great sigh and said it was the one thing he could not leave behind. It was his inheritance, the most precious thing he owns. It was his starter.
EMMA. His what?
MARY. His starter. All bread, you see, comes from a starter. The most common is the yeast you buy in little packets at the supermarket. But it's alive, you know; it's a living organism. And truly great bread comes from truly great starters. The older a starter, the richer, more complex it is. Back when I first started baking, I'd heard tales of starters handed down from generation to generation — ancient starters that had been kept alive for years, for decades! But keeping a starter alive takes time. You have to feed it, watch it, make sure it doesn't die. And this poor man had been tethered to his starter. His father had passed it on to him, made him the keeper of the starter. How could he abandon it? And as I heard this story, I got a strange little tingling feeling in my chest. I heard myself say: "Give me your starter! Let me take care of it!" And as soon as I heard myself say it, I understood that it was nothing less than my heart's truest desire. I wanted this starter. I wanted to bake bread! And I have no idea why, but the man must have seen something in me he trusted. Because he gave me his starter; he gave me the keys to this bakery. And now he is off, traveling the world, just

like he always wanted. And that is how I wound up here, baking bread. Isn't that a marvelous story? *(She laughs.)*
EMMA. And you won't go back to your old life?
MARY. Oh no. Never. I belong here now.
EMMA. You don't ... miss your husband?
MARY. No ... I mean, I think of him. Worry about him, you know. *(The shadow of sadness falls across her face and then retreats.)* But no. I don't miss that life. It's not who I am. I couldn't go back ... it's not just that the door is closed. It's that I don't even know where the door is anymore.
EMMA. Well! *(Beat.)*
MARY. Now. What can I get you?
EMMA. What?
MARY. This is a bakeshop. I assume you'd like to buy some bread?
EMMA. Oh — I'd like what you gave me, please. That was delicious.
MARY. An excellent choice. *(She puts a loaf of bread in a bag and hands it to Emma.)*
EMMA. Oh, there is nothing more wonderful than warm bread!
MARY. So true. *(Emma leaves the shop. The bell tinkles.)*

Scene 3

The Lab.

Emma bursts in.

EMMA. George! I have so much to tell you! *(No one's there.)* George? *(She goes to the doorway and calls.)* George! *(She practices under her breath.)* Mi amas vin! Mi amas vin! *(She sees the machine as if it's been stopped, mid-use. Tapes are scattered everywhere. Emma goes to the machine and presses play. They are voices of different people — different men and women of different ages and cultures. Each says a phrase. The tape goes on and on, phrase after phrase. George enters as Emma is listening to it.)* What is this?
GEORGE. Oh, it's nothing ... *(Emma catches Alta's voice saying,* "Mir ne glessalla.")

EMMA. That was Alta's voice.
GEORGE. Yes. She's part of it.
EMMA. *(Realizing.)* You've spliced together different recordings ... But they're all saying the same thing ... in all their languages, the same thing ... How long have you been working on this? *(George stops the tape.)*
GEORGE. Not long. It's my ... project, I guess you could call it.
EMMA. Is this ... for something, George? Is this for ... Mary?
GEORGE. No, no. How could it be? I don't even know where she is. *(Beat.)* It's funny. I was ... cleaning the other day and I found one of her earrings. There are other things too. I find things of hers, all the time. I find her hairs ... even now. I've cleaned and cleaned. But parts of her. Remain. *(Beat.)*
EMMA. George. Are you ... crying?
GEORGE. What?
EMMA. Your face. *(He touches his face. He looks at his wet fingers.)*
GEORGE. Oh. I've been doing that lately. *(He takes out a handkerchief, dabs his eyes. He recovers.)* Now. What was it you wanted to tell me? *(Beat.)*
EMMA. I like a good cranberry nut loaf. Do you?
GEORGE. What? *(She shows the loaf of bread to George.)*
EMMA. It's hard to find a good cranberry nut loaf. I found this at a new-old bakery in the Upper Midlands. Have you heard about it?
GEORGE. No ...
EMMA. The bread there, it's ... quite extraordinary.
GEORGE. Bread?
EMMA. Yes. There's a woman who runs the place. She just started recently. She kneads the bread herself with this incredibly old starter. And some alchemy or ... I don't know. Energy. Goes into the dough. And makes this extraordinary bread.
GEORGE. Bread ...
EMMA. They say anyone who eats it can't help but fall in love with the baker. George. I think you should go there. In fact, I think you should go there right now.
GEORGE. *(Realizing what she's saying.)* Emma.
EMMA. It's on Carmichael Street. Can't miss it. The Blue Tulip Bakeshop. *(George takes Emma's hands and looks deep into her eyes.)*
GEORGE. Thank you. Emma. You really are ... wonderful. *(He starts to go.)*
EMMA. Don't forget. *(She ejects the tape and hands it to him. He*

goes. Emma sits in front of the recording apparatus. She thinks for a moment. She puts in a blank tape, scoots the microphone towards herself and presses record.) Mi amas vin, George. Mir ne glessalla. Mir ne glessalla.

Scene 4

The Blue Tulip Bakeshop. Mary is in the back kneading bread.

George enters and the door bell tinkles. She looks up with a smile. It falters when she sees him.

A long moment as they take each other in.

GEORGE. I've been looking for you.
MARY. I know. My mother says you call. A lot.
GEORGE. She wouldn't tell me where you were.
MARY. I asked her not to.
GEORGE. Why? *(The answer is painfully obvious.)* You could have become a baker and still been married.
MARY. Oh, George. *(She turns back to her bread. She kneads as they talk.)* So how did you find this place?
GEORGE. The bread … I heard about the bread.
MARY. Ah. And how have you been?
GEORGE. Fine.
MARY. That's good. *(He starts to tear up a little. Mary is kneading and doesn't see it. He recovers. He takes a breath.)*
GEORGE. Mary. Do you know how languages die?
MARY. A lecture, George? Now?
GEORGE. One. Natural disaster. A typhoon, say, knocking out an entire village that is the only place where a certain language is spoken. Two. Social assimilation. When speakers of two languages choose the more socially dominant one to the point where their children speak only that language and lose the other one completely.
MARY. Okay.

GEORGE. I speak many languages.
MARY. Yes, I know.
GEORGE. But I do not speak the one my grandmother spoke. Why? Because my parents didn't really speak it. And didn't care if I really spoke it. Because it was not the socially dominant language. Thus: I never cared to learn it. It was the one language I never cared to learn. And now it's too late. So, Mary. There is a certain language ... our language ... and. If you don't come back, I can't speak it anymore. Do you understand? We are the only two speakers of that language. And if you don't come back, the language will die. And no one on earth will ever speak it again.
MARY. Our language.
GEORGE. For instance, the phrase: "Will somebody please take out the garbage?" Depending on tone it can mean: "You jerk, take out the garbage!" Or, "I feel lonely." Or, "It's our anniversary next week, I hope you remember." Or, "A world without you is unimaginable to me." Mary. Mary. Will somebody please take out the garbage? *(Beat. Beat. Beat.)*
MARY. I'm sorry. But I don't understand what you're trying to say. I have never understood what you were trying to say. *(Beat. George composes himself. He takes out the tape. He lays it on the table.)*
GEORGE. Just a small thing ...
MARY. George ...
GEORGE. Please. Take it. *(She slips it into her apron pocket.)*
MARY. Thank you.
GEORGE. You're welcome. *(George turns to go.)*
MARY. Wait. *(George turns back.)* Here. *(She gives George a loaf of bread. George goes.)*

Scene 5

George holds the loaf of bread.

GEORGE. Every now and then, I have a dream. I dream of Eden. Eden Smith. Eden was the last speaker of Slevitch. She was born in 1912 and she told me once, in one of the great displays of

understatement: "It's sad to be the last speaker of your language." Yes, it is. And then, I start thinking about my grandmother. Even now, years after she died, I can still hear her voice with utter clarity. It tells me things in a tongue that is both as familiar to me as my own face and absolutely incomprehensible. This language, this cacophony, this gibberish, this ... music. My grandmother kept it inside her like a recipe, like a riddle. And to me it made her strange. I didn't like her strangeness ... I separated myself from it and from her the very first chance I could. I've spent my whole life trying to make up for that. I guess I always will. *(He eats a piece of the bread. It is unbelievably good. And somehow, the loss of Mary is made even more profound by the fact that she makes such good bread. A passerby approaches.)*
PASSERBY. Excuse me, excuse me. But what on earth is that heavenly smell?
GEORGE. Bread. *(He gives the loaf of bread to the passerby.)*
PASSERBY. But where did it come from? *(George points.)*
GEORGE. There. *(The passerby goes towards the bakeshop. George goes the other way. The railway platform appears. Emma walks on, holding her suitcase. She glances at a train schedule. She walks along the edge of the platform and cranes her neck to look one way down the track and then the other.)*

Scene 6

EMMA. I decide to go on a long trip. I'm not sure where. I'm not sure for how long. What seems important is simply to go. Anywhere. Somewhere. Wherever as long as it isn't here. *(Emma is on a train platform. The only other person is an old man reading the newspaper.)* Since I'm on a journey and all, I decide to be open to meeting new people. Mary was open to meeting new people and look what happened to her. *(To old man.)* Hello. *(The old man tips his hat.)* I decide to be someone very different from who I am. I'll be the kind of person who strikes up conversations with perfect strangers. *(To old man.)* Nice weather we're having. *(The old man tips his hat.)* Of course, to be that kind of person, it helps if perfect strangers talk back. Well. No matter. I've

brought lots of reading material. *(She opens a book. The sound of a train whistle. Emma takes a seat. The old man is near her. The conductor appears.)*
CONDUCTOR. Tickets. Where you headed?
EMMA. Lower Midlands. Is this the right train?
CONDUCTOR. You're in the wrong car. This is the car for the well-loved. You want the car for the broken-hearted.
EMMA. But what she really said was:
CONDUCTOR. You're in the wrong car. This car doesn't open at Lower Midlands. You'll want to be in one of the first four.
EMMA. Thank you. *(The conductor leaves.)* I'm just about to get up and move to another car when:
OLD MAN. Excuse me? But how are your eyes?
EMMA. My eyes?
OLD MAN. Can you see very well?
EMMA. I can see fine.
OLD MAN. How many fingers am I holding up?
EMMA. Four.
OLD MAN. I'm not holding up any fingers.
EMMA. Oh dear.
OLD MAN. Maybe I should check your vision.
EMMA. *(To us.)* And just like that, he does. *(Emma sits as the old man puts up an eye chart. He sits in front of her with a spoon-like object and checks one eye after the other.)* I don't normally get eye exams from strangers.
OLD MAN. Look up.
EMMA. I've always thought my vision was quite good.
OLD MAN. Look down.
EMMA. Would you like an apple? I brought some with me.
OLD MAN. *Ne dankinde.*
EMMA. You speak Esperanto! U vi parolas Esperanton?
OLD MAN. Speak it? I invented it.
EMMA. *(To us.)* Could this be? Could this man be none other than L.L. Zamenhof, the inventor of Esperanto and my instructor's personal hero?
OLD MAN. None other.
EMMA. *(To us.)* Well, this is turning out to be a wonderful trip so far. But I thought you died.
OLD MAN. To the left, please. To the right. Good.
EMMA. What is your prognosis?

OLD MAN. My dear, I hate to break it to you, but you are going blind.
EMMA. Blind? No.
OLD MAN. Tell me, are you suffering from unrequited love?
EMMA. Yes. How did you know?
OLD MAN. People who suffer from unanswered love often feel as if they are invisible.
EMMA. So true.
OLD MAN. And it is a little-known fact that to be invisible is to be blind. Light, you know, has to bounce off the retina: that's how we see. So if you are invisible, no light bouncing off. Hence: Blind.
EMMA. So what do I do?
OLD MAN. You must fall out of love. Not be invisible. Then you will be able to see.
EMMA. It sounds very simple when you say it. But I've been in love for a very long time. I don't see how I can just fall out of it.
OLD MAN. How many fingers am I holding up?
EMMA. Oh dear. I have no idea.
OLD MAN. Where is this train going?
EMMA. To the Lower Midlands.
OLD MAN. Will I see my family there?
EMMA. You don't know where your family is? *(The old man writes her a prescription.)*
OLD MAN. Lots of rest. Lots of sleep. Fall out of love as soon as you are able. *(He tears it off and gives it to her.)*
EMMA. Zamenhof, the inventor of Esperanto, has given me sound advice. *(The train whistles.)*
OLD MAN. This is my stop. *(He packs up his things. He tips his hat to Emma.)*
EMMA. I watch him go. This great man. *(She moves her seat.)* I move to a different car. And that's when I wake up. *(George is there.)*
GEORGE. Emma?
EMMA. George?
GEORGE. I thought that was you. I just got on. Where are you headed? *(The train is back in motion.)*
EMMA. I'm going to the Lower Midlands.
GEORGE. Why?
EMMA. Didn't you see my note?
GEORGE. What note?
EMMA. In the lab.

GEORGE. Oh, I haven't been back to the lab since ... since I saw you last.
EMMA. Oh. Well, if you must know. I'm going to my mother's and then I'll be taking a trip.
GEORGE. A trip?
EMMA. Yes. A very long one to somewhere quite far away.
GEORGE. And when will you return?
EMMA. I'm not sure. But I'll be looking for a job when I return.
GEORGE. But you have a job.
EMMA. I'm talking about a different job.
GEORGE. You're leaving the archive?
EMMA. Yes.
GEORGE. I thought you liked the archive.
EMMA. I do. But. I think it's time for me to. Move on.
GEORGE. But what on earth am I going to do without you?
EMMA. Oh, you'll manage.
GEORGE. Actually, I don't know if I will. *(Beat.)*
EMMA. Where are you headed?
GEORGE. Nowhere, really. I just like trains.
EMMA. I do too. I like looking at the houses that go by and wondering about the people who live in them. Sometimes it makes me feel sad, I don't know why. *(She looks at George and realizes he's looking at her.)* You must think that's silly.
GEORGE. Not at all. Emma. Isn't there anything I could do to induce you to stay at the archive?
EMMA. To stay?
GEORGE. Yes.
EMMA. Well. I suppose ... *(She glances at the prescription in her hand.)* No. No there isn't. My mind is made up.
GEORGE. But there must be some reason you're going.
EMMA. I'm not at liberty to say.
GEORGE. Well. This is terrible news.
EMMA. It really was more of a one-person operation. I'm sure you'll do fine without me.
GEORGE. No, I won't. I absolutely will not. *(Beat.)*
EMMA. Did you. Did you find that bakery?
GEORGE. *(A moment.)* No. I guess ... in the end, I just decided I wasn't really in the mood. For bread. I don't think I'll ever go there.
EMMA. Never?
GEORGE. No. I don't think I ever, ever will. *(And that is*

momentous. George sits back and looks out the window.)
EMMA. *(To us.)* And then something happens. My vision clears. Oh, it isn't that I'm falling out of love or anything like that. But it's like I can see George, I can see him so clearly. I can see him as a little boy, sitting on the train with his father, without his mother, without anyone else. And I can see how happy that makes him. I don't know how I see all that looking at George, but I do. And you know, I thought I was in love with him before, but that was really nothing. That was really just a warm-up. No. This, this is it. This is love and it is awful and terrible and really overwhelming. *(Pause.)* George?
GEORGE. Yes?
EMMA. Would you really hate it if I quit?
GEORGE. Yes. I really would.
EMMA. Perhaps ... I could stay. A little while longer.
GEORGE. Really?
EMMA. I might.
GEORGE. That would be — wonderful. Emma. Please. It would mean so much. *(The train whistles.)* This is the Lower Midlands. This is your stop.
EMMA. No, actually. I don't think it is. *(They look at each other. The train becomes the lab. Emma takes off her traveling jacket and slips into her usual white lab coat.)* Now, I'm not saying George was motivated out of anything but, well, a desire for things not to change. I mean, it's not like he was in love with me. He was just used to having me around.
GEORGE. Is the equipment ready?
EMMA. And I don't want to say that he'll grow to love me or anything like that. I mean, I'm trying to be realistic here. Even though, lately, I don't know. Maybe it's my imagination. But sometimes it seems to me ... he lingers.
GEORGE. Excellent, Emma. The microphone is working again. *(He looks at her. The look lingers. He turns and starts fiddling with a machine. A voice rings out.)*
EMMA'S VOICE. Mi amas vin, George. Mir ne gles — *(Emma presses stop.)*
GEORGE. What was that?
EMMA. Nothing. Just gibberish. *(She takes the tape. The mail slot on the door opens and a letter shoots in.)* A letter! *(Emma picks it up and hands it to George, who opens it.)*
GEORGE. "Hello good American friends. We have reached our

village safely. Alta was very worry about her garden, but everything seems A-OK, even the tomatoes Alta is very fond of her tomatoes. Resten is weak, getting weaker. But better for him to die at home than in scary white place that smells like steel. *(Emma takes over.)*

EMMA. "Doctor here says time is soon for Resten. But do not be sad, friends. We have live long life full of change and wonder. We are two old people who have been same for a very long time. Started to think maybe we could only ever be same." *(As the letter continues, Alta and Resten appear, side by side. They take over speaking the letter.)*

ALTA. Made us sad, a little. World is change, but somehow we are not change. And we start to think: maybe we are too old for change.

RESTEN. But then, friends, most amazing thing happen.

ALTA. We are on plane home. This time we are not so afraid. We "know the rope," how you say. We squeeze up tiny row and get to seat.

RESTEN. And I say to Alta —

ALTA. Messuh-lass eh-men-arr-esta.

RESTEN. Which mean:

ALTA. "Here, sweetieheart: you take the window." And I say:

RESTEN. Ussamey ver.

ALTA. "No. You." *(They look at each other and beam.)* Now time has become very small, too small for everything we need to say to each other. It is one long conversation and it goes on and on and on. *(Alta and Resten look at each other. They hold hands. They go. Emma carefully folds up the letter and puts it in her pocket. She and George go back to work.)*

EMMA. And I do think of Zamenhof. I dreamed of him one more time. *(The Old Man appears.)*

OLD MAN. And how is your vision?

EMMA. Oh, it's pretty bad.

OLD MAN. Still in love?

EMMA. Still in love.

OLD MAN. Well. There are worse things.

EMMA. Can I ask you something?

OLD MAN. Of course.

EMMA. At the end. When they persecuted anyone speaking Esperanto, when they singled out your children because of what you'd done — did you, at the end, regret it? Did you ever wish

you'd remained nothing but an ophthalmologist and given up your dream of a universal tongue?
OLD MAN. No. No. No. *(The old man smiles and shrugs.)* Because what is language, my dear, if not an act of faith? *(The old man goes.)*
EMMA. And what can I say, except, dankon, Zamenhof, dankon.
GEORGE. U vi parolas Esperanton?
EMMA. Of course.
GEORGE. But I speak Esperanto.
EMMA. I know. That's why I learned it. *(He smiles.)*
GEORGE. Bonege! Do ne parolos in kune, jes? *[Wonderful! Then we shall speak it together, yes?]*
EMMA. Jes. *(George notes the time.)*
GEORGE. The next appointment is here. Are you ready? *(Emma nods. They open the door. Two people come in. Speakers of their own language. The last of their kind.)* Welcome to the Language Archive. How was your flight? *(Lights shift. The Actors come forth, not as their characters, but as themselves.)*
ALTA. Resten lived a bit longer than anyone thought he would and he and Alta bickered lovingly until the end of their days. They didn't die though; they became trees that intertwined around each other so that one would never suffer the loss of the other, and yes, I know that is some old myth and not reality, but that is how I choose to tell it and what's it to you if the last speakers of Elloway are now two trees whose leaves whisper to each other all day long?
MARY. Mary continued to bake at The Blue Tulip Bakeshop. Mr. Baker never returned. She only received a postcard once, from an island off the coast of Greece that accompanied a box of dried grapes. The postcard said, "Feed this to the starter," and she did. The starter continues to produce marvelous bread.
RESTEN. And eventually, Mary listened to George's tape. *(Inside the bakery, Mary plays the tape. She kneads as she listens.)* It was the saddest and most beautiful recording ever made. A symphony of voices that no longer exist, all saying the words, "I love you," in each of their own, doomed tongues. *(Mary starts to cry. Unbeknownst to her, the tears fall into the dough.)*
ALTA. After George's visit, the bread did get noticeably salty for awhile. But even then it was still delicious.
GEORGE. George never did read Mary's last note. Once, when he was a very old man, he came across it. And by then the wounds were so old, that he thought he could bear reading what it had to

say. But upon unfolding it, he found the note was blank. And whether it was blank because Mary didn't write anything on it, or because the ink had faded after so much time, George was never really able to say.

EMMA. George never did fall in love with Emma. They worked side by side for many years, and that was a kind of love. But no, he never did fall in love again.

GEORGE. But on his deathbed, out of all the memories of his entire life, only one came back to him and it was this —

EMMA. It was the time that Emma embraced him after he truly knew, in his heart, that Mary was gone. *(Emma and George. Very gently, he puts his arms around her. Very gently, she puts her arms around him.)*

ALTA. As she holds him, Emma is overcome with joy.

RESTEN. As he is held, George is overcome with grief.

MARY. It is nothing less than the embrace of perfect happiness and perfect sadness. And it is maybe the only time in all of history that two people, despite the fact they are feeling entirely opposite things, actually feel the exact same thing at the exact same moment in time.

ALTA. And it is the one and only time in each of their brief lives —

RESTEN. that they feel utterly and completely —

MARY. — perfectly understood. *(George and Emma continue to embrace. Everyone else goes away. We hear the voices on George's tape saying, "I love you," in every conceivable language. Some dead, maybe some about to be. But whether dead or alive, the "I love you"s continue. They continue for a considerable amount of time. On and on until the lights fade.)*

End of Play

PROPERTY LIST

Book with note inside
Mug of tea with note inside
Dishes
Recording device with microphone
Suitcase
Note
Slippers
Headphones
Large book
Cloth for cleaning glasses with note inside
Book
Tupperware container, fork
Box wrapped in brown paper and tied with string
Bottle of Scotch
Remote control
Tapes
Bowl of dough
Loaves of bread
Shop bag
Handkerchief
Tape
Book
Eye chart with device
Prescription pad, pen
Letter

SOUND EFFECTS

Playback from recording device
Train passing
Bell tinkles
Train whistle

NOTES
(Use this space to make notes for your production)